"Quantum psychology"

"Mix Love"

"Episode #01"

"Honeymoon, which never ends"

Petro Yednak

Publication Date: February 2019

Print Length: 53 pages

Language: English

ISBN: 978-1-7963-7266-3

PREFACE

All people want to feel the love!

When reading my book, you feel the blissful
flavor of love!

You vibrate with a thin note of love!

That book has tremendous inner consistency:

first I talk about love,

then I talk about marriage,

and then I talk about children.

The river of life also flows:

from love to marriage

to children.

CONTENTS

1 HONEYMOON, WHICH NEVER ENDS

Love is never a connection; love is being together.

It is always a river, flowing, never-ending.

Love knows no points; honeymoon begins but never ends.

This is not a novel that started on a certain page and ended on a certain page.

This is an ongoing phenomenon.

Lovers end, but love continues - this is endlessness.

Petro Yednak

This is a verb, not a noun.

If being with someone brings joy, you will
want to experience more and more joy.

If intimacy brings joy, you will want to
explore this intimacy deeper and deeper.

And there are some flowers of love that
bloom only after long intimacy.

There are annual flowers; six weeks they
bloom in the sun, but after six weeks they
leave forever.

There are flowers that need years to bloom,
but there are flowers that need many years.

The more time it takes, the deeper the
love.

But this must be the devotion of one heart to
another heart.

It does not even need to be clothed with
words, because to clothe with words is to
profane.

Mix Love

This must be silent devotion; eyes to eyes,
heart to heart, a creature to being.

It needs to be understood, not to speak.

**Forget about connections and learn to
be together.**

Once you get in touch, you begin to take
the other for granted - and it destroys all the
love stories.

A woman thinks she knows a man, a man
thinks she knows a woman.

No one knows anyone!

It is impossible to know the other, the other
remains a mystery.

And taking another for granted is offensive,
disrespectful.

Being together means that you always
start over, constantly trying to get to know
each other.

Again and again, you introduce yourself to each other.

You are trying to see the many sides of each other's personality.

You are trying to penetrate deeper and deeper into the inner realms of each other's feelings, into the deep caches of the being.

You are trying to solve a mystery that can not be solved.

This is the joy of love: the study of consciousness.

And if you are with someone together, do not reduce this to a connection, and then the other will become a mirror for you.

Investigating it, you will unconsciously explore yourself.

Penetrating deeper into another, recognizing his feelings, his thoughts, his deep currents, you will recognize your own deep currents.

Lovers become a mirror for each other, and

then love turns into meditation.

Communication is ugly, being together is beautiful.

In connection, both its members remain blind to each other.

Just think how much time has passed since you looked into the eyes of your wife?

How much time has passed since you looked into your husband's eyes?

Maybe years.

Who looks into his own wife's eyes?

You have already taken for granted that you know her; what else can you see now?

Strangers interest you more than those you know — you know the whole topography of their bodies, you know how they respond, and you know that everything that happens will happen again and again.

Petro Yednak

This is a repeating circle.

It is not, not quite.

Nothing ever repeats;

everything every day stays new.

Only your eyes become old, only your premises remain old, dust gathers on your mirror, and you lose the ability to reflect the other.

Therefore, I say: be together.

By this I mean a permanent honeymoon.

Continue to explore and go deep into each other, finding new ways to love each other, finding new ways to be with each other.

And every person is such an endless mystery, inexhaustible, incomprehensible, that it is never possible to say:

"I know her" or: "I know him."

At most, you can say:

Mix Love

"I did what I could, but the secret remains a mystery."

In fact, the more you know, the more mysterious it becomes.

Then love is a constant adventure.

Today is the best day of my life!

I, You, Wine, Candy, Flowers, Meeting, Romance!

I have my own religion!

My religion is love!

I and you are friends today!

A month later we got married!

The next is our HoneyMoon!

Celebrate every month all your life!

Question:

"What to do when a husband or a wife deceive?"

Answer:

"Start a new friendship with each other!"

"Interested in each other in a new way!"

"Every day, every week, every month to celebrate a new holiday!"

Well, for now, come on, with you we will break everything that is forbidden to us.

2 PSYCHOLOGY OF LOVE

Man and woman are the doors to God.

The desire for love is the desire of God.

You can understand it, you can not understand it, but the desire for love really proves the existence of God.

No other evidence.

It is because the man loves that God is.

It is precisely because a person cannot live without the love that God exists.

Petro Yednak

A man must move in love.

This is the first step towards God, and it cannot be ignored.

Those who try to avoid the step of love will never reach God.

This is an absolute necessity because you realize your totality only when you are provoked by the presence of another when your presence is amplified by the presence of another when the other takes you out of your narcissistic, closed world under the open sky.

People think that they can love only when they find a worthy person - nonsense!

You will never find this.

People think that they will love only when they find the perfect man or woman.

Nonsense!

You will never find them because the perfect woman and the perfect man do not exist.

Mix Love

And if they exist, they do not care about your
love.

Do not demand perfection, otherwise,
you will not find any love flowing in you.

On the contrary, you will become completely
unloving.

People who demand perfection are not very
loving people, neurotic people.

Even if they can find a beloved or a loved
one, they require perfection, love is destroyed
because of this demand.

As soon as a man fell in love with a
woman or a woman a man, demands
immediately come.

A woman begins to demand that a man
become perfect, simply because he loves her.

As if he had committed a sin!

Now he has to be perfect, now he has to

suddenly throw off all the flaws - simply
because of this woman.

Now he can not be a man.

Either he must become a superman, or
he must become a false, deceiver.

Naturally, it is very difficult to become a
superman, therefore people become deceivers.

They start to pretend, act and play games.

Remember, never demand perfection.

You do not have the right to demand
anything from anyone.

If someone loves you, be grateful, but do not
demand anything - because he does not have
to love you.

If someone loves - this is a miracle, be
reverent before this miracle.

Mix Love

Before you think about how to get love, start giving.

If you give, you get; no other way.

People are more interested in how to grab and get.

Everyone is interested in receiving and, it seems, no one is happy giving. People give very reluctantly; if they give, only to receive, they are almost like businessmen.

This is a deal.

They always continue to strive for how to get more of what they give - this is a good deal, good business.

But the other one does it too.

To love is to share; to be greedy is to accumulate.

Greed only wants and never gives, and love can only give and does not ask for anything in return; it is divided without conditions.

Petro Yednak

Giving love is a real, beautiful experience
because then you are the emperor.

To receive love is a very petty experience
because it is a beggar's experience.

Do not be poor.

At least in terms of love, be emperor,
because love is your inexhaustible quality, you
can give as much as you want.

Love is not a quantity, it is a quality, and
quality of a special category that grows
through bestowal and dies if you keep it.

If you skimp on love, she dies.

If you don't feel jealous, then you will
think that you probably don't love anymore,
and you cling to jealousy because you want to
cling to love - at least love in your mind.

If your woman or your man is with someone
else, and you are not jealous at all,

immediately you start worrying about not loving you anymore.

For many centuries you have been told that lovers are jealous.

Your mind will say:

It's so natural to feel pain if your lover or beloved leaves you because you love so much!

How can you avoid pain, injury, when a loved one leaves you? In fact, you enjoy your own injury, in a very subtle and unconscious way.

Rana inspires you with the idea that you are a great lover, that you loved so much, so deeply.

Your love was so deep that you were shattered because your loved one left you.

Do you feel good or bad?

So, you say: "I want a new red car and I know that I will have it." And then you say, "So, where is she?" I want her for so long, I believed you, but what I want does not appear. "Now you focus not on what you want, but on the absence of the desired, and thanks to the Law of Attraction you get what you concentrate on."

If you concentrate on what you want, you will attract the desired. If you concentrate on the absence of the desired, you will attract the absence (in fact, any object is two: what you want, and the absence of the desired). If you pay attention to your feelings, you will always know what you are concentrating on: on what you want or on his absence, because when you think about what you want, you feel pleasant feelings; and when you think about the absence of it - unpleasant.

When you say, "I need money to lead such a life," then you attract money; but if you concentrate on what you want, but do not have it, think about absence - you repel wealth.

Mix Love

Two people can be very loving together.

The more they love, the less opportunity there is for any kind of relationship.

The more they love, the more freedom there is between them.

The more they love, the less the possibility of any demands, any predominance, any expectations.

And of course, there is no question about any disappointment.

Here is the basic requirement of love:

"I accept the person as he is."

And love never tries to change another person according to his own idea.

You will not try to cut a person here and there to fit him to the size that is created everywhere, in the whole world.

3 POEMS ABOUT LOVE

Someday, we will start waking up
together,

Kisses in the morning, plus your favorite
songs.

We are the main thing that we have!

Everything will come true without any "ifs."

How did we find each other among the
seven billion?

Yes, it was hardly loved at first sight.

Mix Love

Rather, from the first word, see again,

Hear the voice and understand how great it is.

A bit in common, a bit different,

But together we understand how our life is
beautiful.

And going to the "red" will not be scary
together.

You are everything in my life.

Music plays, hands on a waist.

Others fall where we take off.

Where you and I were looking for, others did
not even

Just because we love will not stop.

Without further ado, we merge into a
dance,

And no matter how much you want to stay -

Petro Yednak

Between us again a couple of hours.

Already we miss, we wish you sweet dreams.

Let's not think about anything

In addition to our planet

Drown in unison

Together with our secret

And whatever it is,

Under one sky we

Erasing prohibitions me and you

Let's not think ...

The sun, the warm wind plus the
smiles of loved ones.

Waiting for you, but you do not hurry.

The music is quieter, only birds singing ...

And there are so many happy faces around us!

Mix Love

My heart stops short,

In front of me in a white dress is my bride.

The most beautiful,

And I love you still so much.

The day will come, the ring on the ring finger

And everything that comes after you will like
it.

I saw it all in a dream:

Your tears of happiness and your laugh.

We seem to be forever familiar. Is not it?

And from the first meeting, we seemed to fly.

The world is infinite and we are in it - the
details.

The one and the one that sparkles.

Petro Yednak

Let's not think about anything

In addition to our planet

Drown in unison

Together with our secret

And whatever it is,

Under one sky we

Erasing prohibitions me and you

Let's not think.

Everything will pass, and you will remain -
and for this, there are a million reasons.

I alone can not cope.

I need you.

Our orbits connected.

We see a world that does not exist.

What attracts you like a magnet is no secret to
anyone.

Mix Love

I'm disarmed because I really need you!

I really need you!

The legend is destroyed.

I'm disarmed!

I really need you!

The heart is like fragile glass,

please save him.

To not happen to us,

- do not run away from me.

Our orbits connected.

We see a world that does not exist.

What do you pull like a magnet

- this is no longer a secret

I made up everything myself

Because I love you!

Petro Yednak

Impenetrable fog and snow!

A song of gentle hearts to the chords of rain!

And a happy ending and of course you!

I came to you in the cold and in the heat!

I told you!

I told you about unearthly love!

That you are very gentle and I'm ready for
everything!

Dreamer!

You called me!

Dreamer!

You are smart!

You are beautiful like a fairy!

Well, I, I love more and more!

Mix Love

Like leaves in the wind

Dreams fly,

Like clouds in the sky -

Me and you.

Golden clouds

Float above the ground

Where you are, there I am

My sleep.

I have a dream.

Someday

We will be together, together, together.

O my dream, my dream, my dream,

We will be together,

Someday.

Petro Yednak

We meet with you

Only in my happy dream,

Lips whisper in silence:

"Come to me."

I thought of you

You are the way I want.

I close my eyes,

I'm flying to you.

Do you still love or not?

If in the end, at the end of the tunnel is light.

Do you still love? Just answer.

So that I know whether to burn or not.

Dad - mom

- remember long ago

You told me,

Mix Love

That the "Half" is not easy,

Meet on Earth.

Maybe heaven is not destined.

Maybe just very lucky

But it seems that I found her.

You and me,

- the force of gravity.

Every moment

Like a butterfly inside!

You and me!

So incredible!

And without words it is clear

- I love you!

Petro Yednak

Dad - mom,

- you know, now,

- all around, like a dream.

I want to say, again

that reason is she.

She is,

- my smile on my lips.

I know

what is in heaven now

See the love in my eyes.

Only we two

could understand

all the secrets of heaven and earth!

And reach for the dream,

we could together:

Me and you.

Mix Love

I never went to the beach and did not stand
by the ocean.

I never sat on a sunny beach, burying my feet
in the sand,

But you brought me here, and I'm glad about
it.

Because now I am free, like birds flying
towards the wind.

But here I am, next to you,

The skies are so blue!

I am close to you.

We walked and watched the sun go down.

I would spend the rest of my life standing
here talking to you.

And only we will be in the whole world!

And then I make a wish: swim away with the
fish.

Petro Yednak

We are like waves that roll on the beach and
back.

Sometimes it seems to me that I'm drowning

And you save me.

And I want to say thank you to you from the
bottom of my heart.

This is the beginning of a new life.

A dream come true!

I found my love.

Honey, plunge into this feeling with your
head.

Well, here I found a girl so beautiful and
tender.

Oh, I could not have imagined that you will
find yourself.

Mix Love

Honey, give me that slow kiss because your
heart is all that I have,

And my heart is reflected in your eyes.

Honey, I dance in the dark, and you are in
my arms,

We stand barefoot on the grass, listening to
our favorite song.

When you said you looked disheveled, I
whispered softly,

But you heard that you, dear, you look
flawless today.

I have never met a woman with such a strong
kind.

She shares my dreams and I hope

that one day we will live under the same roof.

I found love

thanks to which I can carry more than the
weight of my secrets:

Petro Yednak

Carry love, raise our children.

This evening of sleepless loneliness.

All thoughts are about you.

I drowned in you.

I want to feel you near.

Honey, do you feel me?

Imagining that I look into your eyes,

I clearly see you.

I imagine you so vividly -

But you are still far away

Like a star

To which I now make a wish ...

Mix Love

As a boy, you call me!

And then hug, and then kiss!

A little watch laugh tick-tac!

Do not regret anything, and love just like that!

4 FORMULAS OF LOVE

Hi, the best!

Thank you for everything!

I give you love!

I'm getting love!

Hi, nice and best!

Thank you very much for love!

I give you my heart, my soul and love!

I deserve love!

Mix Love

Calm my friend!

Peace, bliss!

Calm my brother and sister!

**Peace, love, smile, forgive and you
blessed!**

My friend is the creator!

Make your reality!

You just feel the love that is not sleeping!

My friend - you are the creator, you are God!

Make reality today, tomorrow and in the
future.

Hi, the best!

Let's laugh!

Petro Yednak

I love when you laugh!

I thank you for laughter!

Hello, the best of the best!

Let's smile and laugh!

I love when you smile and laugh!

I am so grateful and happy for a smile and
laugh!

There are no questions in love!

In love there is -

give love!

- I can manage my attention!

Where attention is directed, energy flows
there.

By controlling your attention, you can control
the flow of your life.

5 PRAYERS FOR LOVE

Thank you for my blessing!

I thank for my bliss!

I thank you for my eternity!

I thank for my mind!

I thank for my brilliant ideas!

Thank you for my luck!

I thank for my fairy tale!

Thank you for my good luck!

I thank for my riches!

Petro Yednak

I thank for my health!

I thank for my youth!

Thank you for my beauty!

I thank you for my love!

I thank for my sexuality!

I thank for my tenderness!

I thank you for my kindness!

Thank you for my fun!

I thank you for my joy!

I thank for my vigor!

I thank you for my strength!

Thank you for my progress!

I thank for my omnipotence!

I thank you for my abundance!

I thank you for my freedom!

Thank you for my happiness!

Mix Love

I am blessed!

I am eternal!

I'm smart!

I'm a genius!

I'm lucky!

I'm farther!

I'm god!

I am rich!

I am healthy!

I am young!

I am beautiful!

I'm lovely!

I am sexy!

I'm gentle!

I am good!

Petro Yednak

I'm funny!

I'm happy!

I am energetic!

I am strong!

I am successful!

I am almighty!

I am worthy of plenty!

I am worthy of freedom!

I am free!

I'm happy!

Mix Love

Thank you very much for my love!

Thank you very much for everything!

Thank you for who I am!

The dawn has come, all life awakened!

Living in the sun, my wealth is accumulating!

May it always be that way!

You at home

my expensive money

I'll take care of you

and you call me money.

I care about money

and they love me, and they come to me.

Petro Yednak

My world chooses the best for me.

I am moving with the flow of options, and the
world is coming to meet me.

I myself, by my intention, form the layer of
my world.

My world protects me.

**I am looking for something that will turn
my life into a holiday!**

My world relieves me of problems.

My world cares for me to live easily and
comfortably.

I make an order, and my world executes it.

I may not know, but my world knows how to
take care of me.

**My intention is realized, everything goes
to that, and everything goes as it should.**

Mix Love

Thanks for everything, my beloved world!

Thank you for being there!

6 PSYCHOLOGY OF CHILDREN

Welcome to planet Earth, baby.

Here you can be anyone, to achieve and create anything.

You are the creator and the creator, you are the creator and the creature itself.

You are here for an incredible desire.

There is energy in your body that can light a whole city for a week!

And the choice is always only for you: determine what you want, concentrate on this.

Yes, you will spend a lot of time collecting information, and this is really very important, and you will spend even more time to pass it through yourself, checking its reality and functionality in the script of your personal legend.

And only she will help you decide what you really want.

And no matter how young or old you consider yourself to be at that moment when you are aware of the personal responsibility for your thoughts, and for the answer of your Jin,

who are you

AND ONLY YOU, AND WHO ELSE ISOLATED FROM THE BOTTLE?

Incredible power will awaken in you.

And the world will bend.

And the eyes and the feelings inside you will
suddenly become so loud

that voices and opinions from the outside just
squat down with their mouths and eyes open.

Your children are not children to you.

**They are sons and daughters of the
longing of life for itself.**

A child is not a thing.

You can not own a child.

Speak:

"This is my baby" means

uphold your ignorance.

Children come thanks to you, but not
from you,

And although they are with you, they do not

belong to you.

You can give them your love, but not your thoughts,

For they have their thoughts.

These small sentences are amazingly significant if you understand that a child is longing for life on its own.

It means,

that the child is closer to the true source of life,

then the oldest person.

The old man is close to death.

Petro Yednak

Continuation in the next episode ...

ABOUT THE AUTHOR

Petro Yednak
Date of birth:
June 23, 1984
Citizen of Ukraine.
Permanent residency Poland.
Lawyer since 2005
Psychologist since 2010
Writer from 2015